The Verses On Witness Consciousness
By Sadguru Kedarji

The Verses On Witness Consciousness

Copyright © 2016 by Sadguru Kedarji

All rights reserved. No part of this book may be used or reproduced by any means, graphic, electronic, or mechanical, including photocopying, recording, taping or by any information storage retrieval system without the written permission of the publisher except in the case of brief quotations embodied in critical articles or reviews.

Copies of this book may be ordered through booksellers or by contacting:

The Bhakta School of Transformation
330-623-7388 Ext. 10

NityanandaShaktipatYoga.org

ISBN: 978-0-578-38070-4

Printed in the United States of America

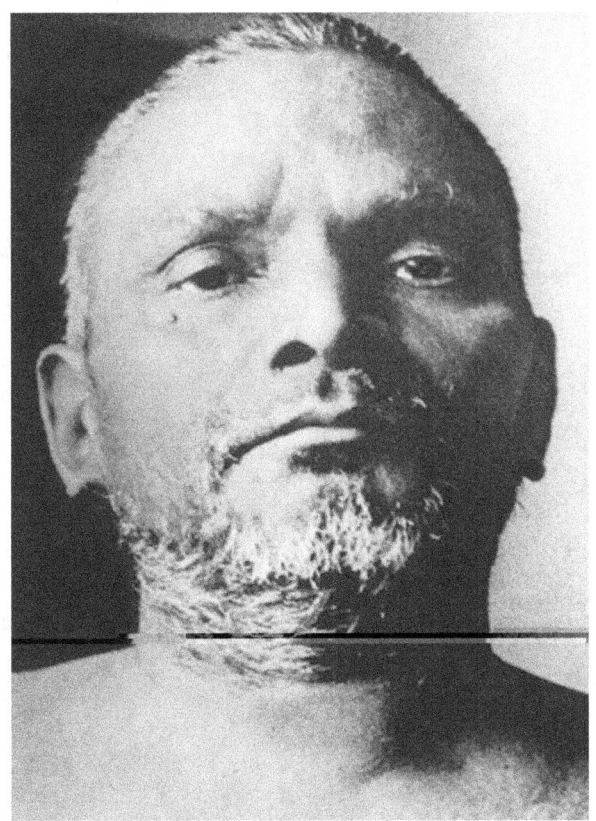

*Shri Bhagawan Nityananda of Ganeshpuri
The Master of Kedarji's Lineage*

Contents

Introduction   vii

The Verses On Witness Consciousness   11

Introduction

I offer these verses at the lotus feet of Shri Bhagawan Nityananda of Ganeshpuri and Lord Shiva, the Guru of the Siddhas. To *That* Shiva-Shakti Principle be the glory.

The challenge to your experiencing permanent spiritual transformation, and the ultimate state of Liberation that follows, is this: Invariably, you spend your time concerning yourself with comfort, security and reward before finding out who your really are. If, instead, you discovered your true nature in order to cure your amnesia, a Reality full of Grace and Blessings would unfold for you. In this way, finding your true wealth inside you will surprise you with an exemplary abundance that you already own!

For so many lifetimes you have chased after comfort, security and reward, embodied in the pursuit of pleasure, in an attempt to avoid pain. Indeed, this has resulted in the constant search for liberty and happiness where it is not. Consequently, you are always looking outside for what is not there.

My Master used to tell the story of the musk deer. The musk deer carries the wonderful scent of musk in its own navel. And yet, when it smells that scent coming from inside itself, it follows the breeze that carries the scent into the mountains, searching for where the scent is coming from, thinking it to be somewhere outside itself.

It runs and runs after that scent, following the breeze up into the mountains. It runs and runs and eventually dies trying to find the source of that scent. Then the people living in the mountains cut open the musk deer and remove the musk! Until you find the true source of your happiness and peace, you are like that musk deer. So, get smart!

Above all, a restless mind cannot produce the kind of

Peace, Joy, Centeredness and Happiness that is essential for individual well-being and the collective well-being of everyone on the planet. Holistic well-being requires a mind that is free from agitation, worry, doubt, fear, anxiety and restlessness.

Inside you there is an ocean of Peace, a wellspring of Joy and Inspiration that never runs dry. To experience this, you have to go beyond your mind and beyond your senses to that *Witness* to your mind and your senses.

This begins by making the mind quiet so that you can experience what we call your natural, free state of being, your True nature. So, a quiet mind is essential.

What if you could experience a silent mind and then no thoughts whatsoever, followed by a wonderful experience of Peace and Joy, **in less than three minutes**?

Further, what if you had a simple, daily practice in which you could maintain this experience of a silent mind, while making your mind sharper? The purpose of what is taught in this book is to give you that experience.

My Shri Gurudev has said that there are many journeys in life, but that the journey to Liberation begins with the understanding *Shivo'Ham*, I am Shiva, I am the Self. This highest of understandings is imparted by the sages of steady wisdom of my lineage.

Without reaching for and embracing it in the present moment, it is impossible to stay the course long enough to face yourself. And facing yourself is done to root out the karmic obstacles to your Freedom and Liberation. These are obstacles that you yourself have created. They prevent you from retracing your steps back to God.

Flushing these obstacles out in order to burn away all that you are not, requires that you be tested. Indeed, these tests that are given by a living Sadguru, provide the proof of the absolute power of our approach and practice of Witness Consciousness Centering.

For this reason, I offer these verses to help all seekers understand the huge benefit of practicing Witness Consciousness Centering to experience the state of the Observer, the Witness to everything. This offering is made so that you can do so in a way that you understand and experience the following; That all the aspects and expressions of Humanity actually belong to the Self, not to the false notion of individuality, not to the body.

This book will offer an introduction to our approach, *Nityananda Shaktipat Yoga*. This Siddha Science emphasizes the importance of the *Pure Perceiving Awareness* that comes with the practice and experience of Witness Consciousness Centering, coupled with the practices of meditation, chanting, selfless service and contemplation.

Siddha Science is the science that has been crafted and tested by the Siddhas, the Self-realized Love Beings of my lineage. This Siddha Science has been molded in the laboratory of their existence, dating back to the pre-bronze age.

Therefore, I ask that, just for a while, as you read and contemplate these verses, that you set your cynicism aside. Set what you think you know aside. Set your ego aside and set your current life experience aside so that you can contemplate these verses with an open heart and mind, ready to receive.

What we seek is beyond language. However, language is necessary to convey understandings that lead to the Truth. In a recent program one man said, "I was raised Catholic. My mother will never accept that I am God." So, please try not to get hung up on certain terms. They are 'educational' terms designed to direct your attention within.

Instead, do whatever it takes to get your feet into the water so that you can begin swimming in the ocean of your own Bliss, the Joy and Love of the true Heart.

If you are having trouble with the references here that you are God or the Self, then you can begin with the understanding that *it is possible* that you are much greater than you think you are. At the very least, I encourage you to start there, if it makes it easier for you to listen and imbibe.

May All Be Joyful,

Sadguru Kedarji

The Verses On Witness Consciousness
By Sadguru Kedarji

"You are the one witness of everything, and are always completely free. The cause of your bondage is that you see the witness as something other than this."
~ Ashtavakra, from his Ashtavakra Gita

1. Witness Consciousness or the State of the Observer: An experience in which you are able to watch your thoughts, emotions, notions, etc. come and go passively, without judgment and without any reaction or response that allows the energy of egoism to arise. A state in which, from that Witness to your mind, you are able to observe that Source from which all thoughts rise, are sustained and withdrawn.

2. The purpose of practicing Witness Consciousness Centering is to begin the important process of *Remembrance* as you go about your daily, mundane activities. The great beings tell us that Remembrance means resolving one's identity crisis by identifying with the Self, with our True nature. To do so in every movement of thought, emotions, notions, etc. in our Consciousness is to experience the Witness to your mind.

3. Why do you need to be reminded? Because you forget who you really are. Through so many karmas (mental conditioning) of so many past lives and the present life, you have developed the false notion that you are just a person, a mere individual, that you are the body with an exclusive personality, that you are small, ordinary or delightfully weird. Without remembering who you really are, without being reminded constantly that you are the Self, there is no hope for permanent spiritual transformation. Finding true peace and happiness then becomes a fading dream, mostly due to the raging river of worldly distractions.

4. We know when we are thinking but how do we know we

are thinking? How do we know we have slept? How do we know we have dreamt? We know because there is a higher power, a power that we refer to as *the Knower, the Witness, that Supreme Principle* that is beyond the mind and beyond the senses. *That* is what observes these changing states of experience. That Witness is who we really are.

5. Reaching for this Witness Consciousness state, with practice and the Grace and leadership of a perfected spiritual Master, leads to your awareness merging in the experience of the Witness. In Shaivism, this merging is referred to as *Pure Perceiving Awareness*. It is a Blessing of the Grace-bestowing power that flows through a Shaktipat Guru. This Blessing also comes by way of your Grace inherent in your performance of instructed spiritual practice.

6. To begin to understand and to experience this State of the Observer known as Witnessing Awareness, it is necessary to hold and to contemplate the fundamental teaching of our approach. This is a Shakta approach (upaya) leading to the Shambava state. It is elucidated by Shivaji in such sacred texts as the Shiva Sutras and the Spanda Karikas.

7. This instruction is framed in the utterances of the great beings of our lineage who state, **See God In Each Other. The Self Exists Equally In All.**

8. In order to practice and perfect Witness Consciousness Centering, we begin by holding the highest understanding "I am Shiva. I am the Self. I am God."

9. Even if you have not yet gathered the evidence of this Truth, by way of direct experience, you can hold this

understanding, this wisdom. It will help you gather the evidence of this fact by allowing you to build a foundation for going higher. This occurs with the spiritual practice and leadership in application of this instruction that will become the proof of this Truth.

10. Without embracing the understanding "I am Shiva. I am the Self. I am God," it is impossible for us to sustain the practice of Witness Consciousness Centering long enough to shatter belief and opinion in the direct experience of the Highest. We hold this understanding, coupled with our spiritual practice as instructed by a Sadguru, to prove this statement to ourselves, in the laboratory of our own existence. **Holding this understanding becomes our act of Grace.**

11. Therefore, the great beings tell us "You are not a person. You are the Self. You are God."

12. In fact, your perfection is already with you. The great travesty is that you *forget* who you really are. You lose awareness of the Self, the Pure Perceiving Awareness of your own Divinity. *You lose this awareness by concealing from yourself the fact that you are the Self.*

13. The great beings tell us that the culmination of the spiritual journey rests in the experience of *never forgetting* our True nature as the Self, even when thoughts and fancies play in the mind. The point of following the instruction in the practice of this state of the Observer is *to become established in this experience of remembrance, of never forgetting.* The instruction is an act of the Sadguru's Grace.

14. Repeated here as a reminder. ☺ Perfecting the state of the Observer is a practice of *Remembrance*. We have to

practice remembering who we really are because, through lifetimes of useless mental conditioning (our Karmas), we are in the habit of forgetting. We forget by way of embracing the false notions that we are the body, the senses, a mere person, that we are an individual, a personality only. And we have plenty of worldly distractions that cause us to engage in this amnesia.

15. Due to these Karmas that are the foundation for our mental conditioning, we need to be constantly reminded of the Truth. "I am Shiva. I am the Self. I am God." Of course, without the Grace and daily spiritual practice that allows us to prove this in the laboratory of our own existence, we never make progress. We can't shatter the illusion of lifetimes of the mental conditioning that keeps us bound, that keeps us believing that we are small, that we are just ordinary, that we are sinners, impure, unable to change.

16. The greatest challenge to the destruction of the Karmas that keep us entangled in what is false is how to keep our Humanity. This challenge is in how to enjoy living without remaining bound. Walking through the prison gate into the Total Freedom that comes from knowing, through direct experience, who we really are is essential.

17. This is a matter of resolving an identity crisis by inner investigation and experience – beginning with the experience of Witness Consciousness. STOP HERE FOR A MOMENT AND TAKE A DEEP BREATH. It is recommended that you use the following link to experience the practice of some centering methods that will help you prove the import of these verses to yourself. https://nityanandashaktipatyoga.org/dharanas.html

18. All thoughts, notions, emotions, etc. rise and fall from the same source. Everything in the world of forms is a superimposition, a projection into Consciousness. Some

superimpositions free us, others keep us bound. It is the nature of the Divine Conscious energy (also known as Shakti) to manifest, sustain and withdraw, thoughts/notions and emotions in our Consciousness. Therefore, it is the nature of the mind to think. This is why the great beings tell us, "Make the mind your friend by turning it within."

19. Beyond the movements in Consciousness of thoughts, emotions, etc. is the source and power which threads through these functions. When you lay hold of this power amidst the movement of thoughts, feelings and emotions in your Consciousness, you will cease to identify with these as who you are.

20. By the power of your *witnessing awareness*, you will realize that there is no difference between 'happiness' and 'sadness.' You will realize that the notions of 'happy' and 'sad' come from self-appropriating movements in Consciousness to the false notion of individuality, to the false notion that you are the body, just a person, place or thing.

21. In truth, these are the same sensations arising out of the Self, being sustained by the Self, and being withdrawn back into that very same Self. God alone is. It is the Shiva-Shakti power alone that gives the experience. That power alone is true and worth our highest reverence.

22. In this way, even when your level of interacting with others must differ due to the varying roles you play, your inner experience does not shift away from that of the Witness, that Knower. In turn, this becomes the experience of your own sweet Joy, the Bliss of the Self. This is, first and foremost, an inner experience.

"These sense activities of mine may, in their Joy, have full play in their objects. In the midst of sense activity, may I never lose, not even for a moment, not even slightly, the recognition of identity with thee. May all this become a blessed sacrament to this true identity."

~ *Utpaladevacharya*, from his Shiva Stotravali
  (Meditations On Devotion to Shiva)

"In the court-yard of duality, the Self, the Shakti of the Supreme, of its own accord, threads through everything. When this fact is realized and experienced from moment to moment, as duality and differences appear to widen, the inner experience of Unity becomes stronger. In this state, the enjoyment of senses objects only reinforces the experience of the highest Bliss, as one is reminded, over and over again, that sensory enjoyment belongs to the Universal Experient, the only doer, the highest cause – that all these are Divine expressions of that Universal Experient."

~ *Jnaneshwar Maharaj*, from his Amrithanubava
  (Nectar of Self-Awareness)

These utterances indicate what it's like to live in *The Paradise of the Heart*, a place that you can reach, with the practice that includes the heightened awareness brought about by Witness Consciousness Centering.

Useful definition: *Doership* – the act of *self-appropriating* the movements in your Consciousness (thoughts, notions, emotions, sensory experience and all the rest) to the false notion that you are a person, an individual, the body; instead of acknowledging that these movements belong to the Ultimate Cause or Reality, the Self.

23. The great beings tell us that life is a precious gift that should never be taken for granted. It is a rare privilege given to transform ordinary perception into the Divine vision of a Heart full of Love and Light.

22. Life is the stage on which the amazing unfolding of *The Play of Divine Consciousness* takes place. And life is the stage for realizing our True nature in the moment, from moment-to-moment, in the transforming Love of the true Heart. This Paradise of The Heart is a *Pure Perceiving Awareness* that you can easily merge in. It happens by way of the practice of Witness Consciousness Centering. It is an abode of Love *without distinctions*.

23. The Self-realized beings tell us that it is entirely possible to Love all in the same way, without making distinctions in this Love, even as we engage in varying and changing levels of interacting due to the roles we play in those various interactions. In fact, nowhere can we find a saint, Siddha or holy being who instructs us to find or make distinctions in Love. *Quite the opposite.* This is because, in the abode of the true Heart, these distinctions don't exist. *There is just Pure Perceiving Awareness.*

24. Of the experience of Pure Perceiving Awareness, someone recently shared that, upon experiencing it, she wanted to remain there. *She never wanted to come out from that experience.* This is how you know that you have merged in the state of Witness Consciousness. You feel like you never want to come out of that state of indescribable Joy. This approach, along with the instruction and practices offered in Nityananda Shaktipat Yoga, exist to help you become established in this state.

25. Our approach, that begins with the practice of Witness Consciousness Centering, is not offered to give you what

you already have. *This approach exists to help you burn away what you are not.*

26. There are varying degrees of *witnessing awareness*. These correspond to the various stages or levels of manifestation (the Tattvas). The best way to become anchored in the witnessing awareness of the Observer is to practice Witness Consciousness Centering *with the highest understanding that you are the Self.* To engage this practice with the understanding that you are the Ultimate Reality or Cause that *plays* at thinking, that *plays* at the expression of emotions, that *plays* at experiencing and expressing Humanity through the senses is the highest form of Meditation.

27. This is what ensures that the energy known as egoism cannot form in your Consciousness *in the moment* of that *Remembrance* of who you really are.

28. You can practice this Remembrance, moment to moment, by avoiding the act of *self-appropriation*. Again, we define self-appropriation as an act of concealment that occurs when you self-appropriate movements in Consciousness such as thoughts, notions, emotions, cravings, limiting desire based on the false notion that you are just person, etc.

29. In other words, when you self-appropriate in this way, you allow the energy of egoism to form in your Consciousness. This is where it begins. You lose the Witness Conscious state in that moment. You *forget* you are the Self and that the movement in your Consciousness is an expression of the Self, the God-principle. This causes you to contract. If not arrested, you come to believe this contraction to be who you are. *In this way, you actually make yourself small.*

30. To avoid doing this, there is the practice of Witness Consciousness Centering that is engaged to experience the state of the Observer or Watcher. This practice, that leads to the experience of Pure Perceiving Awareness, is exercised in order to prevent the energy of egoism from forming. You may find it helpful to stop here and revisit the practice of the centering methods on this page
https://nityanandashaktipatyoga.org/dharanas.html

31. Prove to yourself that this is entirely possible with practice. If Kedarji can do it, if the great beings have done it, anyone can. If you practice preventing the energy of egoism from forming, even as thoughts, emotions and notions may play in your mind; *if you practice this from moment to moment,* you will experience the state of no ego, if even for a moment or two. And if you can experience that for a moment or two, you can have longer and longer glimpses of no ego, over time, with practice. Then you reach the point where you realize that egoism can be transmuted and, ultimately, retired in the growing realization that you are the Self *playing* at the expression of your Humanity.

32. Everything is a conjoining of energies in Consciousness. These energies are aspects of one Divine Conscious energy that we refer to as Chit Shakti or Mahashakti. Some of these energies keep us bound, entangled in the false notion that we are just a person. And some of these energies free us, liberating us from the imaginary ignorance we have created that keeps us small and contracted. The practice of Witness Consciousness Centering that leads to the perfection of *Pure Perceiving Awareness* is the gateway. The gateway to what? To our embodiment in the freeing energy of *Grace* that causes us to rise, to awake to the Abode of the Heart.

33. Spiritual life cannot be sustained without unconditional Love (a Love without distinctions that already exists inside us). It cannot be sustained without the experience indescribable Joy that is unbreakable. This is the purest place within us that reflects light, love, compassion and forgiveness everywhere. Going to this sacred place within is how we *remember* the Self. It is how we *remember* the Truth; that Love, Peace and Joy are who we really are. This is the only way to permanent spiritual transformation. The state of the Observer allows us to begin experiencing this indescribable Joy of the Self.

34. This is the beginning. Hold this understanding while going about your daily mundane activities/ Hold it while repeating your mantra, while meditating and chanting. Embrace it while doing whatever it is that you believe is living, so that you can experience true Humanity, true living that is *independent* of contraction. This true Humanity is free of limiting desire, attachment, attraction and aversion. It is independent of the movements in your Consciousness that *appear* as thoughts, notions, emotions and all the rest.

35. To support your practice of Witness Consciousness Centering, there are some things you will need to do in order to continue to expand your awareness in this state of the Observer.

36. A house without a solid foundation will get swept away with the tide. You don't want that. In addition to practicing Witness Consciousness Centering, as shared in some of these verses, you are encouraged to meditate daily. This helps build a foundation for deepening your inner experience of Witness Consciousness while going about your day. Chanting is also very good. Even if you chant the Mantra *Om Namah Shivaya* for just 10-15 minutes each day, you'll find this to be very helpful in anchoring you

inside. Attracting Grace to your practice and your life by doing so is also important.

37. The Self-realized Love beings of our lineage all say that one should meditate, chant, contemplate and perform selfless service knowing and affirming the secret: When we sit for meditation, we *should not* sit with the understanding that we are a person, an individual attempting to meditate in that moment. *Instead*, (for example) when we sit for meditation, we should hold the understanding that this is God meditating on God, that we are the Witness to whatever takes place in our meditation. If you have chosen a living Sadguru (true spiritual leader), meditation on that beings' form is also very helpful in anchoring you in meditation on the Self as the Self.

38. When we chant, the great beings tell us to chant with enthusiasm, affirming that we are the Self, chanting our own name. The holy beings plead with us to approach all of our daily spiritual practices in this way, with the understanding that we are that Observer, the only doer, who is experiencing and expressing our True nature in the form of that very practice.

39. This helps us to avoid the identity crisis by breaking the habit of self-appropriation that causes us to believe we are the doer. The ego is an energy that forms in your Consciousness, causing you to believe that you are not the Self, but that you are the body with an individual identity and personality, that you are just a person. These false notions lead to a state of contraction in which you come to believe in doership. This keeps you bound to ever-increasing Karmas.

40. Reminder: ☺ The energy of egoism forms when you self-appropriate what you are experiencing in the moment

to what we call the small "i," the notions that I just mentioned above.

41. Reminder: ☺ In the Witness Conscious state that leads to the experience of *Pure Perceiving Awareness,* you can engage and experience thoughts, emotions, the senses, and all the rest, without engaging in this act of self-appropriation. *In this way, the energy of egoism cannot form.* Over time, with practice, you can eliminate the ego energy from your Consciousness altogether.

42. In fact, this is what our approach is all about. In Nityananda Shaktipat Yoga, we eliminate the thoughts, notions, ideas, beliefs, opinions, attachments, attractions and aversions that otherwise keep you bound. Being bound is being contracted in a way that you don't *remember* and *recognize* your True nature, The Self, in each moment. We reach for the state of the Observer to begin freeing ourselves from the false notions that cause us to forget who we really are.

43. Whether you believe the ego can be *destroyed* or not doesn't matter. Whether you believe the ego can be *eliminated* permanently or not doesn't matter. Your companion in a living Sadguru has to use educational terms to help you direct your mind in such a way that it will relish in dissolving in the ocean of Peace inside you. So, please don't get stuck in an intellectual argument about this.

The fact is *you can* prevent the energy of egoism from forming in your Consciousness from moment-to-moment, by reaching for the state of the Observer or Witness. *Prove this to yourself in the laboratory of your own existence.* Then there will be no intellectual argument. Then you will realize that, if you can prevent the energy of egoism from forming in the moment, you can expand on that prevention to make that experience more lasting.

Because change can only occur in the present moment, this is where we practice mastering these energies, by not allowing the energies of dullness or contraction (like the false notion of individuality) to form in the moment. Over time, with this practice you can attain the state of the Self-realized beings.

You can reach a state where you realize that you are that Ultimate Reality or Cause that has taken birth as this world of forms. You can realize and experience that all movements in Consciousness are Divine enactments in the Play of the Shakti. *This realization will create a space in you that will allow for your adjusting your life and actions accordingly.*

Na Shivam Vidyate Qua Chit. It means *nothing exists that is not Shiva* (The Self). With this understanding, we can allow what comes in the moment to merge in the Consciousness that we are. Then, gradually, every experience and interaction takes us back inside to revel in the Joy of the Self.

Then all activity becomes non-activity because there is no act of self-appropriation that would otherwise cause doership (the energy of egoism) to arise. Prove this to yourself, over and over again, in the laboratory of your own existence, and watch what happens next. There is *more*, and you can find out what *That* is for yourself. Spiritual leadership is also necessary. So, contemplate these verses for a while.

You are all great beings, the Self. You are perfect. Your perfection is already with you. You just need to break the age-old habit of concealing this fact from yourself.

Obstacles to Practicing and Experiencing Witness Consciousness

Judgment while engaged in your practice (example):
You sit for meditation and you immediately begin to meditate on the thought "I can't meditate." That's a judgment, a false notion. If you can watch your thoughts come and go, you can meditate.

Better choice:
Observe the thought "I can't meditate." Observe it passively like watching a scene in a movie. Don't react. Don't respond. Witness the movement of this thought as it rises in your Consciousness, remains there for a short while, and then dissolves - either of its own accord, or due to the rising of another thought that you are witnessing. Now. Observe that place from which this thought "I can't meditate" rises. Now witness the point or place in which this same thought dissolves. You can even replace that thought with the inward repetition of the mantra *Om Namah Shivaya* (I am Shiva, I am the Witnessing Awareness).

Another More Useful Choice:
Let's say that you sit with the thought "I'm going to meditate now." Or you say, "Okay, I'm going to *try* to meditate for a short while." Instead, affirm to yourself "I am The Self and I'm going to meditate on The Self now. I am God meditating on God. I am Shiva. I am Shakti. Shakti is going to meditate on Shakti now."

Then, as you are meditating, maybe the thought arises, "My mind is too busy. This is taking too long. The mantra is not working. I need coffee." Avoid meditating on this thinking. For example, try not to react with something like "Damn it. Why am I thinking of coffee when I should be repeating my mantra?!" Instead just observe the thought "My mind is too busy. This is taking too long. The mantra is not working. I need coffee" *passively*, until it passes. This is meditation. If you observe your thoughts passively in this way, your mind will slow down and become quiet. In our approach, this is known as *Savikalpa Samadhi*. If you can watch your thoughts, you can practice Witness Consciousness Centering. And if you can practice Witness Consciousness Centering, you *can* meditate. With the right instruction and practice, your meditation will deepen.

You can also be present with the Shakti, as in recognizing the thought as an expression of the Divine. Example: "Oh Shiva how playful you are. You think of coffee when you should be repeating your mantra. How divine is your play! What entertainment. I'm just going to watch. *Om Namah Shivaya*." The reason this is effective is that, by attributing your thoughts to the Shakti, by understanding them as movements in Consciousness, you immediately direct your mind to *the Self* in that moment. In other words, you remember who you really are as your mind is placed back on contemplating the Absolute.

This is the Blessed Sacrament that you should seek to make with your thoughts and actions. Remembrance of your true nature is everything. *Due to your karmas, you have to be constantly reminded of the Truth.*

48. Outcomes belong to God, the only Experient. Choose not to self-appropriate the experience of your interactions to the false notion that you are just a person, the body, a personality. Instead, practice remembrance of your True nature. Remember that you are the Self and that all other people, places and things are the Self also.

Here is another example of a centering method you can practice while engaged in daily activity, to move you

back into the sublime state of *Witness Consciousness* that is indicated in the above verse.

The purpose of this example is to help you demonstrate to yourself how you can use any interaction with a person, place or thing as a centering method to experience your True Nature and the essential nature of everything and everyone as the Shakti, the Self.

The following are the lyrics to a wonderful song by Roger Daltrey (youtube.com, Roger Daltrey + Without Your Love, will get you to a recording of the song. It's not the original, but still enjoyable)

This was one of my favorite songs for many years...still enjoy it today, but in a greater way.

You can show me the way
Give me a sunny day
But what does it mean without your love

If I could travel far
If I could touch the stars
Where would I be without your love

Whenever I get to feel down and out
I think about what you said, and I give out

If I could fly away, if I could sail today
Where would I go without your love?

You can show me the way
Give me a sunny day
But what does it mean without your love
And if I could travel far, if I could touch the stars
Where would I be without your love?

And if I ever wander away too far
You come looking for me with open arms

I could forget my home
Feel like a rolling stone
But who would I be without your love

And what does it mean without your love
Where would I be......

Certainly just reading the lyrics, and listening to the song will probably cause pleasant feelings to arise in you in association with a person, place or thing. Maybe someone with whom you have derived or love, believing that love to have come from that form or that person. Or maybe the pleasant feelings will be due to the wonderful artistic expression and writing of Roger Daltrey. Or maybe the song will bring up a memory of someone or something you feel you have lost.

Better Choice:
If either of these feelings or thoughts arises in connection with the lyrics, be with your feeling *long enough to witness it without judging it,* but not long enough to dwell on it. Instead, relish in offering these notions to your witnessing awareness as movements in Consciousness, expressions of the Divine.

Another Useful Choice:
Recognize that Roger Daltrey is also the Self. He is God, a Divine expression of the Ultimate Reality or Cause, and not a person. The song and its lyrics emanate from the same source your Mantra rises from. The song is withdrawn back into that same source. It is, therefore, a movement in Consciousness, just like all your other thoughts; An expression of the Divine -- that Witnessing Awareness that

is the one and only Universal Experient. You can affirm this to yourself and then watch what happens.

Better yet, you can prove the above statements to yourself with yet another useful choice.

Take one or two verses of the above lyrics and repeat them inwardly and quietly to yourself, *but do so without allowing the thought of or any images of people, places and things to form in your mind.* Instead, as you stop repeating the lyrics, allow them to become a sensation and follow that sensation back inside to its source.

Practice this over and over again until you are able to repeat a verse or two without images of people, places and things forming in your mind. And then continue the practice until you are able to let go of the verses in your Consciousness by just observing them passively and allowing them to dissolve. Reminder: ☺ What is left after all thoughts and notions dissolve in your Consciousness is who you really are.

OR

Logon to Youtube.com and find the song. Play it with your eyes closed. Listen to the song *with full attention and awareness.* Be present with it but, again, do not allow your mind to associate images or thoughts of people, places and things with what you are listening to.

Instead, witness what is taking place in your Consciousness, *passively*, as you listen to and enjoy the song. Beautiful song, isn't it. But why is it beautiful? *It's beautiful because Shakti is there to recognize its beauty.* Ah! Attribute your enjoyment of this song to that Shakti and, as the song ends, focus on the sensation in your

Consciousness that the song dissolves into, and follow that back inside.

If you run into the following thinking....
"I can't listen to the song or enjoy the lyrics without believing that it's the song that is giving me a pleasant feeling." Or "I can't listen to the song without remembering my boyfriend, wife, husband, lover, dog, cat, son, daughter or the people who I value as friends because they give me the pleasure that I want." Or "I've been thinking of my mother for the entire song. This isn't working. It's a ridiculous exercise!"

These are all *judgments* -- useless commentary on what just took place in your Consciousness. *Unless* you simply *Observe* this commentary passively, while remembering that you are the Self and that they are part of your Divine play. In that moment you will recognize who you really are, even if just for a moment. And this is beneficial because, with practice, one moment of this recognition expands into another and then another and then another. *Om Namah Shivaya*!

These are some examples of how to practice Witness Consciousness Centering in the waking state or in sitting for meditation, where we choose not to self-appropriate the experience of our interactions to the false notion that we are just a person, the body, a personality. Instead, we remember that we are the Self and that all other people, places and things are the Self also.

49. Forgetting this fact in the moment causes the energy of egoism, the energy of contraction or limitation to fester in our Consciousness. This leads to our superimposing or projecting this contraction on to others. Then we fault-find, we judge, we make distinctions in love that conceal true Love and Compassion from our experience. We have the

choice, in each moment, of not allowing that limiting, binding energy to form in our Consciousness by reaching for the witnessing awareness that reminds us of the source of all that is – that Ultimate Reality or Cause that we are.

50. A question may arise at this point: If we are God, if we are so pure, why is the mind so busy? How did we come to believe that we are small, just a person, an individual, the body with a name, just ordinary, a sinner, strange or weird?

51. **Karmas.** All embodied beings have karmas created in many past lives and the present lifetime. The great beings tell us that our life in this world is influenced by the consequences of our actions performed in many previous lives, and that every soul experiences the fruits of his/her karmas. The *creation* of Karmas doesn't stop until one becomes completely established in the *Pure Perceiving Awareness* of the Absolute that allows one to master inactivity in the midst of activity.

The karmas that have already begun to bear fruit (known as prarabdha) still manifest and have to be faced. Even the Self-realized beings have prarabdha karmas to face. The unenlightened have both latent karmas and manifested karmas to face. Add to this the karmas that continue to be created out of the doership that comes from thinking and acting out of identification with the body/individuality, rather than the Self.

52. For the purpose of increased understanding and awareness, the holy beings tell us that karmas are the mental conditioning that we have created over so many lifetimes of believing ourselves to be something or someone other than the Self. In other words, we create this mental conditioning (karmas), by self-appropriating movements in Consciousness (our thoughts, feelings, emotions and all the rest) to the false notion that we are a

person, the body, just an individual, ordinary, strange or delightfully weird. This is an act of concealment that allows the energy of egoism (doership) to form in our Consciousness.

53. *Superimposition.* You can't recognize what you don't know. An Alzheimer's patient develops amnesia and can't even recognize his/her closest family members. The false notion of being a person, an individual, the body, etc. is like this amnesia. You can't recognize the highest when you have forgotten what that looks like. You have traded that memory in for a kind of fantasy or illusion about who you really are.

This illusion is part of the karmas that dictate your mental conditioning, how you think, who and what you attract to you. These karmic tendencies also determine what you project or superimpose into Consciousness and on to other people, places and things. There is no way around this *until* you come to *know* your True nature.

54. Until we become *established* in *Pure Perceiving Awareness*, we consider ourselves to be small, just ordinary, a person, strange, etc. This is what we come to know as who we are. In the state of contraction or limitation, this is what we recognize. And what we recognize, we project or superimpose outwardly on to other people, places and things. All we can do with what we *don't* recognize through direct experience is to form an opinion or belief about it....**based on what? Our mental conditioning; Our karmas. There is no way around this.**

55. This mental conditioning (karmas) is the sum total of all the impressions left behind on your mind and deposited into your memory from your past lives and the present life. *Until you are released from these karmas, these impressions are what you know, what you are able to*

recognize. They are familiar, comfortable. **And you are attached to what is 'comfortable' because you pursue comfort and security rather than pursuing the direct knowledge of who you really are.** *You chase after what you want, instead of wanting to know who you really are.*

56. Furthermore, until you practice Witness Consciousness Centering long enough to become *established* in Pure Perceiving Awareness, here's what happens. These karmic impressions, your karmic patterns, *will cause you to think and superimpose in a way that you will not recognize that you are superimposing*, **because the cause of that projection is at work just below your conscious awareness.**

Until freed from these karmic patterns, there is no way around this either, *unless* you have a spiritual master who can help you attain a more useful and freeing projection (example: "I am the Self, the Witness who observes the play of these karmas and offers them to the fire of my own Joy."). Then, once you perfect Witness Consciousness Centering by resting on your Pure Perceiving Awareness, there is no need to superimpose any longer. The mechanism of superimposition itself is dismantled.

Examples:
Suppose someone pleads with you in a way that you find small or distasteful, because pleading is something you don't recognize as being useful, or maybe you find it distasteful because it's not something you would do. Maybe you don't like apologizing or maybe you find impassioned pleas to be 'soupy dramas.' These are all examples of *judgment* or *superimposition*.

How do you know that the person pleading with you is not *simply trying to reach you,* to inculcate compassion and mercy in you to encourage you to get into your heart? You don't, unless *you* have had this as an experience that is an expression of true Love without distinctions, that one Love of the Abode of The Heart.

Or, suppose you decide that you are right and the other person is wrong. How do you know that you are 'right' and the other person is 'wrong?' How did you come by this perception?

A story about superimposition: When I first met my spiritual leader, my Guru, I observed that, at times, he was indrawn and appeared to be aloof. I perceived this as arrogance. Then I observed him expressing emotions that I also expressed. When I observed him being human in a way that I was used to, I thought him to be just a mere, flawed, egotistic person (because this is how I perceived myself, so I reflected this outwardly on to others).

I did not know his inner state because, at that time, I had no experience of Witness Consciousness or Pure Perceiving Awareness. So, I assumed (superimposed on to him) that his inner experience of Humanity must have been like my experience of Humanity at the time; That when he expressed emotions like sadness, excitement, or when I observed him being affectionate, chummy or expressing himself in ways that made him appear to be ordinary (from my own experience of what expressing those was like), I projected on to him my limited experience of what I knew those to be. I superimposed that he must be sliding into contraction.

My Gurudev was a practical joker -- but in the way that he used practical joking to reach certain people with an important message. I also had a love for practical joking at that time.

However, when I engaged in practical jokes, I did so in order to laugh at others, to be amused at their expense. This caused me to become cynical and sarcastic, qualities that kept me bound to the false notion of individuality, while increasing my lack of faith and distrust in others.

So, when Baba engaged in practical joking, I perceived that was the same as when I engaged in practical joking. I projected that his motivation and inner experience were like mine, that he was just ordinary. So, for a period of time after we first met, due to my superimposing, I lost respect for him because I did not know that I was projecting these on to him. It was all taking place *beneath* my conscious awareness, of which I had very little.

I chose to find fault in him (and to find fault in others who very well may have been having an inner experience from a higher awareness than I knew to be possible). Later, I was blessed by His Grace with the instruction and leadership that gave me the experience of Witness Consciousness.

Then I myself began to recognize, from that direct experience of inner knowing, that *the expressions of Humanity can be profound sources of Bliss*. And that great Joy can be a continuum of experience derived from movements in Consciousness *that are attributed to the Shakti*, that are understood as Divine expressions of the One Universal Experient or Cause.

57. Therefore, the great beings tell us that there is the need for experiencing the witnessing awareness that allows us to stop judging and fault-finding, *long enough to deepen our understanding of what is actually taking place in our Consciousness during experiences of both 'comfort' and 'discomfort.'* Comfort and discomfort are perceptions that manifest out of the false notion of being just a person or

individual. Both are actually movements in Consciousness, expressions of the Shakti or Divine Conscious energy of the Absolute.

(Note: Understanding roles is important. For example, the fact that a parent has to correct his/her child in the process of preparing that child to lead his/her life *is not* fault-finding. It is the parent's role and duty, as part of properly preparing the child for life. In the same way, the spiritual mentor or companion in the living Master has this same duty to students/devotees, in preparing them to attain permanent spiritual transformation. This *is not* fault-finding.)

58. The Self-realized beings say that, if your witnessing awareness is not sufficiently developed to the point where you are able to slip into the experience of Pure Perceiving Awareness on a regular basis, you will not know that you are the Self. You will not experience the Truth; that you are *playing* at thinking, *playing* at the expression of emotions and all the rest. **And, if you don't know, from direct experience, that you are the Self and not a person, you will superimpose limitation and lack on to yourself and everything and everyone around you. This includes superimposing your own weaknesses on to the great beings.** *There is no way around this.*

59. The great beings frame this fact in this way so that we begin to embrace how vital it is to practice Witness Consciousness Centering during our daily spiritual practice. This is a practice that includes consciously going within (meditation, chanting, contemplation, prayer), as well as sustaining the practice when we are interacting with people, places and things in the waking state. In this way, we stop thinking of ourselves as small so that we to stop enabling our amnesia! Indeed, we are able to go beyond beliefs and opinions that are based on the mental conditioning dictated

by our karmas, in order to experience what is waiting for us on the other shore.

60. The Self-realized beings tell us that we have been going in the wrong direction for a very long time. Because this is the case, they say that we have to go (away) for a while, so that we can return. Go so that you can return. They mean that you have to *remove the distractions* to your practice of what is mentioned above (our daily spiritual practice and the unfolding of our spiritual lives) for a good period of time.

This is done to create boundaries of solitude around you, *long enough to be able to change your direction permanently*. This is akin to turning the runaway train around so that you get on the right track, so that you can transform your ordinary perception. Then you can return with a new vision, a Divine vision of a Heart full of Love and Light.

61. This Love is too great to settle for just a fleeting glimpse. The practice of Witness Consciousness Centering leads to absorption in *The Abode of The Heart* and changes how you are vibrating.

62. The power and practice of Witness Consciousness Centering is a power that heals from within.

Reminders:

Witness Consciousness or the State of the Observer: An experience in which you are able to watch your thoughts, emotions, notions, etc. come and go passively, without judgment and without any reaction or response that allows the energy of egoism to arise. A state in which you are able to observe that source from which all thoughts arise, are sustained and withdrawn.

The purpose of practicing Witness Consciousness Centering is to begin the important process of *Remembrance*, while engaged in spiritual practice, and as you go about your daily mundane activities. The great beings tell us that *Remembrance* means resolving one's identity crisis by identifying with the Self, with our True nature, in every movement of thought, emotions, notions, etc. in our Consciousness.

The ego is an energy of the illusory aspect of the Shakti (also known as Shiva's Maya). And it *is not* always present in your Consciousness. The ego manifests at the moment you self-appropriate a thought, feeling or notion to the small 'i,' your false sense of individuality or the false notion that you are the body. If, instead, you attribute everything that floats through your Consciousness through the energy of the mind -- if you attribute everything to the Shakti – thereby recognizing all of it as a *play* of Divine Consciousness, a *vibration* of the Self, then, in that moment, the energy of egoism cannot form.

63. The Self-realized beings tell us that *The Self* is the great actor. *You are That*. For example, in *playing* at the expression of emotions, it's not that these are not felt. It's a matter of understanding *who* feels and *where* that which is felt is actually taking place.

64. Who is feeling it? Who is experiencing it? The individual? (your perception that you are just a person?) or *The Self*? Your understanding of this makes a difference in whether or not *what* you are feeling causes you to contract or allows for increased awareness of the Highest in the moment, from moment-to-moment. The Self-realized beings tell us that understandings always dictate feelings. Therefore, we reach for the understandings that allow our Bhakti (devotion/longing) to increase. Then we are able to

embrace our heightened awareness by *recognizing* Grace, rather than *sabotaging* Grace.

Experience Share: As just one example, I want to share an experience with you that I hope will help you understand and imbibe the importance of verses 63 and 64 above.

In the past, I have had a recognition well up within me of how much I miss interacting with a being who I had kept very close to me. We no longer have this interaction.

In the moment of the experience of this feeling of *missing*, I welcomed the appearance of the form of this being into my Consciousness, remembering this being as a gift of God's Love. Then I offered the feeling to *That One* who experiences (the Observer), by way of my witnessing awareness. *What remained is what is always there for me, the nectar of Self-awareness known as Bliss or Joy.*

Then the feeling of *missing* this manifestation of Love began to form in my Consciousness again. Only this time, I stopped the act of manifesting at the level of sensation and did not allow the thought of this person's form to manifest in my Consciousness. *Again,* what remained is what is always there for me, the nectar of Self-awareness known as Bliss or Joy.

"For one who has attained wisdom, sweeter even than 'the bliss of Liberation' is the enjoyment of sense objects (people, places and things)! This enjoyment *is not* experienced in the notion of individuality and limiting desire. It is experienced in the palace of Bhakti (devotion) where (in the abode of the Heart) that Lover and God experience their sweet union."
    ~ Shri Jnaneshwar Maharaj, from his *Amritanubhava*.

So, whether I welcomed the thought of this being into my mind or not, the *Pure Perceiving Awareness* of the Absolute remained. In fact, this was also my experience, as well, during the time of our interacting when we kept each other's company. This is the experience that Shri Jnaneshwar is referring to in the above quote.

It can be understood in another, simple way. Let's say you *love* gourmet coffee. If this is the case, you'll probably partake of any gourmet coffee, having the same enjoyment, even though you 'prefer' the company of 'dark magic' over 'Italian roast.'

In this way, you can begin to understand the Bliss of the nectar of constant Self-awareness in daily life. The gourmet coffee is like the Bliss that is the constant substratum. The preference of one type over the other is like making the choice of one aspect of the same Shakti over another…like choosing a higher vibration of that same Shakti over a more contracting one.

I had mentioned earlier the practice of perfecting Witness Consciousness Centering that causes the experience that answers the questions *Who is feeling it? Who is experiencing it?* This practice will help you understand and know that, as you become established in the experience of Pure Perceiving Awareness, whether you have thoughts, feelings, sensual movements in your Consciousness or not, it will not change your inner state.

While interacting with people, places and things, or when reflecting on those interactions – it doesn't matter and will not matter. *Once <u>established</u> in this highest awareness, you will realize that nothing can be added to it and nothing can be taken away from it.*

Then you will be free to engage in your Humanity without the energy of egoism or the false notion of individuality forming in your Consciousness. This experience is one of relishing in the conjoining of your Bhakti (devotion and longing) with objects of sense, out of your inner knowing that people, places and things are reflections (movements) of the Divine. This is the import of Jnaneshwar's verse.

It is as Lord Shiva stated to Parvati, "Lokhananda Samadhi Sukham." The Bliss of this world is the ecstasy of Samadhi.

This takes some practice.

65. There is a heart chakra, and then there is the triadic heart of Shiva in the *Sahasrar*, the highest spiritual center. The great beings tell us that God exists in our feeling, and that the understandings we hold dictate how we feel. Some feelings free us to experience our own Bliss, others keep us bound to making distinctions and creating differences that keep us entangled. The feeling in the heart chakra is offered up to *Sahasrar*, with the *understanding and experience* of the Witness. *This allows for the experience of a pure Humanity that becomes freeing, not binding.* The Humanity becomes freeing by way of your realizing that your essence is eternal Joy and that your interaction with people, places and things causes your Devotion to this Joy to expand.

66. The Self is *independent*, not interdependent or dependent on anything or anyone else. *And you are That.* This *does not* mean that we are not all interconnected, *because we are.* But not by way of the binding, false notion that we are individuals destined to pursue happiness through our attachments to and interactions with each other. **We are interconnected by the God-principle, by the Equality Consciousness established due to The Self existing equally in each of us.** Being interconnected in this way allows us to nurture each other *in each other's Grace and the highest Love of the pure Heart*.

Shri Bhatta Narayana, a great saint of Shaivism, states, "I adore you, O Lord, who creates the *erroneous* perception of duality and distinctions for those who are deluded by the world, only to destroy that false perception for those who want to know the Self. You thereby, veil and unveil the Bliss of direct experience that is beyond dichotomies."

67. Your perfection is already with you. You are perfect. You are That. This is what the holy beings say. When will you embrace this fact? When will you begin to see that, in perfection there is more perfection, *by ceasing to look for imperfection in perfection* - by discarding what is limiting, binding and contracting for that which is the perfection that you are? We answer these questions by way of our practice of Witness Consciousness Centering.

The state of the Observer allows us to watch how we are vibrating *so that we can raise our vibration to match our True Nature.*

68. An actor *plays* at his or her role. In time, the actor may become a master actor, by perfecting his or her craft. And yet he was always *playing* at his role, right from the beginning, *bringing out what was there from the start.* Your perfection is like this. Look for it where it is by removing the veil that you use to conceal it from yourself. Then embrace it. Embrace your purity. Embrace the Light. Swim in that Love. Increase your feeling, your longing for That, *so that your Devotion burns away all that you are not.*

69. In perfection there is more perfection. Reach for it. Don't settle for less than you already are. You are That One who watches this perfection unfold. See this Truth there inside yourself *and adjust your life accordingly.*

70. The great beings tell us that human beings cannot live without Love. When we recognize that this Love is the

Highest Reality or Cause, that it is the same Love that has caused the Universe of forms to come into being, we can gain great strength from its purity and unconditionality. The strength gained from this Love allows us to honor each other as The Self, as God, *regardless of the differing levels of our interaction with people, places and things that may be dictated by our various roles.*

If we allow our karmas to be permeated by this Love, those karmas cannot negate or destroy this Love. Then we can repeat the mantra, *Om Namah Shivaya* (I am the Self), with the strength of this Love. This Love is all there is. The state of the Observer causes this recognition and experience to unfold.

71. When you remain steady in the experience of The Witness, thoughts can be there or not. Emotions can be there or not. The senses can have their play (or not). You remain steadfast in your remembrance that you are the Self and that it is this very Shakti that directs your senses, your thoughts, your feelings, your emotions. It doesn't matter what the nature of the thought or feeling is. *These belong to God.* In this way, you can engage in true Humanity while avoiding the entanglement of doership, by not allowing the energy of egoism, the identification with the body, the personality or the senses to form.

72. Then you can make even your 'personality,' with all its expressions, *a blessed sacrament to the Lord.* Then you don't have to judge yourself or others. Then you won't fault-find or criticize others. A person expresses sadness, remorse, anger, pity, etc. How do you know what that person's inner state is? How do you know that the person is or is not entangled in doership? Why judge? Why find fault?

73. *If you look hard enough for faults in others, you will find them, even when they are not there.* This will cause

your witnessing, spiritual awareness to contract and contract. Instead, gather the evidence for yourself that what I share here is entirely possible by experiencing it for yourself. Again, you do not have to be Self-realized in order to have these experiences of heightened spiritual awareness and Bliss in the moment. And what you begin to experience in the moment can become a more steady experience, over time and with some practice.

I suggest that you stop here again, for a few minutes, to practice some of the Witness Consciousness Centering techniques here
https://nityanandashaktipatyoga.org/dharanas.html

74. *It is true that, in many cases, one's attachment to gain/loss, comfort, security, reward and attraction (with respect to people, places and things - worldliness) must suffer a major setback in order for people to desire true Freedom.* Even though this may be the case with you, the state of Liberation or Self-realization is not a matter of destroying the mind. It is not a matter of criticizing or judging the emotions or the experience of the senses. And it is not a state in which the experience of these is avoided or 'negated.' It's a matter of choosing a higher, purer vibration, of which the essence is Joy.

75. Even the phrase 'destruction of the ego' is an *educational* term since, in the final state of Liberation, one realizes that the 'ego' does not exist. In the meantime, egoism is an energy that does not have to be allowed to form. The lotus flower sits in the mud of the pond, yet remains clean, the dirt and muddy water running off its beautiful leaves. In the same way, without the experience and perception of The Self threading through all of the qualities/expressions of Humanity, the experience of Bliss, of your own sweet Joy is not complete. Becoming anchored in *Pure Perceiving Awareness* becomes the proof of this.

76. One can be blessed with the experience of *Pure Perceiving Awareness* by following the practices instructed by a living Master who bestows Grace; practices that include, for example, Witness Consciousness Centering, meditation, chanting, japa and selfless service. The purpose of meditation and the chanting of Chaitanya (live) mantras is not to judge or criticize thinking or the experience of the emotions or the senses. The purpose of these practices is to discard thinking when it is not necessary in order to make the mind quiet enough to experience the state of the Observer that becomes the Pure Perceiving Awareness of the Absolute.

77. This Pure Perceiving Awareness is the very nature of Bliss or Joy that is eternal. That Joy is the Self, your True nature.

78. This is a state in which Humanity and the experience of being human can be expressed freely without the energy of egoism forming in your Consciousness.

79. Here's how. *Daily spiritual practice* ☺ -- the kind of practice that the Self-realized beings use to realize The Self.

80. To be clear, the ego idea, the false notion of individuality, is a formidable obstacle to overcome on the spiritual journey. *The poor ego morphs in ways that one attached to the false notion of individuality cannot recognize.* What the Self-realized Love beings say, that the only thing to be renounced is egoism, is absolutely true. This is not an easy task and the renouncing requires being led with instruction. But it is not so difficult to experience if practiced from moment to moment. This can be practiced in a way that gives you a growing experience that the ego can be renounced and retired, for good, even in the midst of thoughts and the expressions of Humanity.

81. From the study of the teachings of the Saints of our approach, we know the limitation of the ego to be an energy of perception in Consciousness. It is one of the 36 stages or levels of manifestation (Tattvas) that are spoken about by the great masters of Trika Shaivism.

82. Everything is a movement of energy in Consciousness. In our approach, this movement is known as *Kriya*. This movement is an aspect of the One Divine conscious energy we call *Shakti*. This Shakti has two aspects; *the immanent and the transcendental*. In our practice of Witness Consciousness Centering, we learn to transmute the immanent aspect into the experience of the transcendental, *by attributing everything to the Shakti*.

83. We do this by avoiding the act of self-appropriation. Again, in Nityananda Shaktipat Yoga we define self-appropriation as an act of concealment that occurs when you self-appropriate to the false notion of individuality (personal power). The movements in Consciousness such as thoughts, notions, emotions, cravings, limiting desire to the false notion that you are just a person, an individual, the body, a personality, the sum total of your experiences, just ordinary, small, a sinner, a weirdo – when you attach yourself to these are who you are, that is self-appropriation.

84. In other words, when you self-appropriate in this way, you allow the energy of egoism to form in your Consciousness, *by your own power*. This is where it begins. You lose the Witness Conscious state in that moment. You *forget* you are the Self and that the movement in your Consciousness is an expression of the Self, the God-principle. This causes you to contract. If this habit is not arrested, you come to believe this contraction to be who you are. In this way, you actually make yourself small.

85. To avoid doing this, the practice of Witness Consciousness Centering or the state of the Observer that

leads to the experience of Pure Perceiving Awareness, is exercised in order to prevent the energy of egoism from forming. This practice of increasing your witnessing awareness is applied to both the daily spiritual practice you engage in with eyes closed (such as sitting meditation), as well as to the state you practice at maintaining, as you go about your daily mundane interactions with people, places and things.

86. If you can prevent the energy of egoism from forming, even as thoughts, emotions and notions may play in your mind; If you are instructed well in practicing this from moment to moment, you will experience the state of no ego, if even for a moment or two. And if you can experience that for a moment or two, you can have longer and longer glimpses of no ego. Then, over time and with practice, you can reach the point where you realize that egoism can be transmuted and, ultimately, retired in the growing realization that you are God.

The light bulb carries the name 'light.' However, this is a misnomer. A light bulb parades itself as if it is the giver of the light. But the bulb has no power of its own to give or do anything. Without the electricity that runs to that bulb, the bulb is useless and has no power. It is the Universal energy called 'electricity' that actually gives the light. For without that energy there would be no light.

In the same way, just as there are no individual doers, there is no such thing as personal power. There is One power only. We call it the Shiva-Shakti power that gives power to all the forms, that is the power of perception of those forms, and that also withdraws those very forms. This One power is the *energy substratum* of everything and everyone.

That power is the giver, the taker and the receiver of all Blessings, all Grace and all Knowing.

For more information about programs, events, courses and retreats to strengthen the practices and awareness spoken of in this book visit

        NityanandaShaktipatYoga.Org

www.ingramcontent.com/pod-product-compliance
Lightning Source LLC
Chambersburg PA
CBHW071846290426
44109CB00017B/1938